# Her Own Words

## A Liverpool Mother's Life

Veronica Kay

TEXTWORKSHOP

First published in the European Union by textworkshop.

ISBN: 9798298528139 (paperback)

ASIN: B0FMQ3CKD8 (ebook)

Cover photograph: © Robert C. Ryan
Design by: Sabina Ostrowska

For permissions or enquiries, please contact:
Robert C. Ryan

Cortijo Berruguilla

18270 Lojilla

Montefrio

dr.robert.ryan@gmail.com

*This little book is based on a series of handwritten notes by*
*Veronica Witham, née Kay (1913–2007)*
*Liverpool*

# Contents

# Introduction

*H*er Own Words: A Liverpool Mother's Life* by Veronica Kay is a work of unassuming literary and cultural significance. At first glance, it appears to be a simple, unvarnished memoir; a modest handwritten record of one woman's recollections of a long and difficult life. But on closer reading, it reveals itself to be something far rarer. It is a document of lived literature composed out of an instinct to preserve memory. 'Accidental literature', one might naïvely say. Veronica Kay's prose is existentially precise and the events that she records are never over-explained. Why waste fifty words when ten will suffice?

Spanning the greater part of the 20th century, Veronica Kay's memoir is written in language that is immediate, colloquial, and deeply authentic. Her style is neither ornate nor self-consciously crafted. Its literary merit arises from its restraint. In prose that is unadorned and emotionally direct, Kay captures the texture of her everyday life in Liverpool with sharp narrative clarity. Her diction is plain, but her emotional cadence is unmistakably powerful at moments. Often, a single sentence or paragraph distils decades of hardship, love, endurance, or sorrow. These moments possess an economy of expression and an emotional compression that gives her memoir its quietly devastating power.

What distinguishes this text from other memoirs is not only its candour but its narrative voice, which is wholly consistent and unmistakably hers. Veronica Kay writes not to entertain. Instead, she bears frank witness to her own life, to the choices and losses she endured, and to the survival of her family through poverty, war, motherhood, and emotional estrangement. How could that be entertaining? However, her narrative is at once intensely personal and broadly representative since it offers insight into social and domestic conditions rarely chronicled with such honest immediacy and from such a grounded perspective.

From an academic standpoint, *Her Own Words: A Liverpool Mother's Life* offers material for readers interested in working-class literature, oral history, feminist autobiography, and social realism. Thematically, it traverses the terrain of economic precarity, gender roles, emotional resilience, and generational memory. Yet it never descends into melodrama or moralising. It is precisely in its refusal to dramatize the events of her life that the text achieves its modest strength. Veronica Kay's reflections resist gauche sentimentality. Instead, the reader is presented with the raw truth of lived experience, unfiltered and unrevised. In this sense, the memoir aligns with traditions of oral testimony, domestic realism, and working-class autobiography.

To read *Her Own Words: A Liverpool Mother's Life* is to encounter a voice that is simultaneously ordinary and extra-ordinary. In giving shape and form to memory, Veronica Kay gives voice to a generation, and in doing so, she invites us to consider the value of stories told not by celebrities, but by every-day individuals, dear family members, who have endured.

# Foreword

Some people leave footprints in our hearts so deep that the passing of time will never erase them.

My Nan was one of those people.

This book is a tribute to her: to the strength she showed in the face of life's many challenges, to the grace with which she carried herself, and to the love she gave so freely to everyone around her. It is a record not only to what she endured, but to who she was: a woman of deep resilience, sharp wit, and endless heart.

Nan didn't have an easy life. She knew hardship, sacrifice, and sorrow; more than her fair share. But she never let those things define her. She rose above them, not with loud declarations, but with steady strength and quiet determination. Her warmth could fill a room, and her stories – often laced with wry humour – were always told with a sparkle in her eye and a life-lesson lurking not far beneath her words.

As her granddaughter, I feel incredibly proud to be able to share some of the memories that still live so vividly in my heart. Time spent with Nan and Granddad was full of love, laughter, and the kind of comfort only a grandparent's presence can bring.

I remember staying over at Nan's house when I was a little girl. She'd lay out her softest blankets on the box-room bed to make me comfortable, and an electric fire would be glowing a warm orange in the corner of that small room. Downstairs, we'd have toast and a cup of tea before bed; hers always with a little more sugar than she let on. Then she'd tell me a story, often about her own childhood in Liverpool or proud tales of her brother Robert, who died in the War. I'd listen with wide eyes. Even the sad stories had warmth in them because of the way she told them; always with personal meaning, always with an open heart. Then it was, "Up the dancers and in to bed with yer, young lass!"

Another of my favourite memories was being in her kitchen, sleeves rolled up, helping to make her famous potato cakes. She'd let me shape them (even when they were wonky), and we'd eat them hot, fresh off the pan, with butter melting into them. It wasn't just simple, homemade food; it was love made manifest. I can still taste them now.

And then there was the chocolate bars. Nan always had a large bar of Cadbury's Dairy Milk stashed under her bed mattress. I wasn't supposed to know it was there, but of course I did. I'd sneak out of bed of a morning ever so quietly, when she was downstairs in the kitchen, and go hunting for it. I think she knew I'd nicked the odd square all along. She just pretended not to notice. That was her way. Gentle. Kind. Always letting you feel like you'd got away with something naughty, just to have a shared secret.

I also remember Uncle Ted's mischief and my aunties chatting in the front room, and how Nan somehow magically managed to be at the natural centre of any social gathering by dint of her calm and knowing presence.

My cousin Robert recently researched the military records of her beloved brother, L/Cpl Robert Kay of the Black Watch, who lost his life in combat in WWII. His ultimate sacrifice and the subsequent heartbreak it brought to the Kay family informed the indomitable woman she came to be. Such are the momentous events that constituted the fabric of her life. Her bravery, love, loss, and an unwavering sense of duty.

This small book is not just a recounting of what she went through. It identifies her as the heart of our family, a steady anchor in any storm and a quiet, appreciative presence that filled our happiest memories.

As you turn these pages, I hope you feel her presence, too. I hope you hear her voice. And above all, I hope you understand the legacy she left behind.

This is her story – and it deserves to be told.

Letitia Roberta, her daughter and my mum, always had an amusing story to share about Nan. Nan's kindly spirit remains with us through those stories.

With all my love and gratitude,

*Lisa Williams* (Granddaughter)

*Photo 1. Lisa and Nan*

*Photo 2. Veronica Witham (née Kay), newly married*

# My Life
## Making Out by V. Kay

The year is 1989. I am 76 years of age when I write or try to write this, 58 years of my life. I promise to write the truth as far back as I can remember.

W ell, it was the year 1930, the 3$^{rd}$ of December, when I left my Mother's house to marry Edward Witham, who I had only known for ten months. He was tall and older than me by ten years. I fell for him. I really didn't know him or what I was letting myself in for. But them days, and at 17 years of age, we knew very little. I was brought up strict. Do as you're told. No freedom.

So that's why I left home, unknown to my Mother, as I thought that she didn't know I was getting married.

But she did know.

*Photo 3. The Liverpool Cotton Exchange Building on Old Hall Street, which housed the Liverpool Registration Office for marriages in the 1930s. The building was originally constructed in 1905–06 in an Edwardian Baroque Revival style. It opened on 30th November 1906 with a ceremony attended by the Prince and Princess of Wales.*

*Photo 4. In the late 1960s, the exterior of the Liverpool Cotton Exchange Building was demolished and redesigned. The building was re-named 'Cotton House' in 1969.*

So, when I came out of the Registry Office, I was shocked to find her and my sister waiting outside. My Mother had never met the man I had just married. I walked up to her, while the man I had just married turned away and walked off with his mate and my, then sister-in-law, Marie.

My Mother looked at me with such hurt and anguish on her face, and mad as a hatter at what I had done and <u>who</u> I had married. She said God will punish you for the hurt and upset I had caused. I started to cry.

I said, "I'm sorry Mam."

She said, "You don't know what you have done, you stupid child. You don't know what you have let yourself in for."

I did not understand those words at the time. But it did not take me very long to find out.

So, after saying, "Sorry Mam", I walked away and went to join my Husband and company.

My heart felt heavy. My eyes full of tears. My wedding day. One I will never forget. My Mother didn't want to know me anymore. What had I done?

"I was soon to find out."

My Husband took us back to his Mother's. She had a bit of a spread for us. As for me, I could not eat. All I did was cry. That was one day I will never forget. Also, I had told the man I married that I was going to have his child, which was untrue. So, my Husband did not marry me because he loved me.

I soon found that out.

Well, the day I got married, we had nowhere to live. So, my sister-in-law and I went looking for somewhere to stay, which was a furnished room. [It] consisted of a bed, table, two chairs, sofa, and some dishes. The rent was ten shillings a week. Gas and lights you paid as you used it. No cooker. A small fire-grate to cook on. No cooking utensils.

Of course, my Husband and his mate got drunk. So, it was not a happy Event. Next day, my Husband gave me a few shillings to buy a couple of pans, soap, towel, and some food.

So, my married life began.

My Husband was a man of few words. I thought he had a job. Such a job. I was soon to find out. Loading coal at one shilling a ton. He used to earn enough to give me half a crown a day, 12 ½ pence.

He also drew the dole, which was twenty-six shillings a week. Man and wife! He had enough money in his pocket every night to go out boozing. While I stayed in!

Well, in nine months and ten days later, I became the Mother of a little girl, who I called Audrey.

By that time, my Mother had repented. But she still hadn't met my Husband, [not] until I had had the baby, and I asked him to go and let my Mother know I was alright.

But they were not friendly.

*Photo 5. 1933 [marked on the back of the photograph] Mrs Veronica Witham and Mr Edward Witham outside Cheshire Lines Committee building, Ranelagh Street, Liverpool. Opened 1874, demolished 1973. Photo probably taken by a Liverpool [candid] street photographer operating near Central Station.*

While I was pregnant, we had to move house; no children allowed. Went to another furnished room. Much nicer. Very clean. Bed linen was nice and white.

So, it was there that I carried my firstborn. I remember I had been to see my Mam in the afternoon. But I was restless. So, I went home about three o'clock. My water broke. I remember being confused. Did not know what to do. I lay down on top of the bed. I must have dozed off when my Husband came home. He took me to the Hospital and the next day, twelve fifteen, I gave birth. Eight pounds, two ounces, little girl. I was in Hospital for ten days, and then my life began. I was eighteen years of age. I had to manage to look after the baby.

They taught [me] in Hospital how to hold the baby when you bathed it. So I got on alright. I was happy with my baby, and my Husband got an extra three shillings a week for the baby. So that meant twenty-nine shillings a week for three of us. I suppose I should have counted myself lucky. I was getting an extra ten shillings off my Husband for loading coal. So, the amount weekly then was thirty-nine shillings a week, to pay out rent twelve shillings, gas eight shillings a week, food and <u>clothes</u>. Of course, I had to go around the second-hand shops for those.

All too soon, fifteen months later, I gave birth to a son, six pounds thirteen ozs. with red hair, where Audrey was dark. They were two beautiful children. The boy, I called Edward, after his Father.

I remember Ted coming into the Hospital to see the baby. He looked at him and said, "Where does he get the red hair from?"

I said, "I don't know."

He laughed. The joke was on me. I had red hair.

Well, two children to look after and, wait for it, another three shillings for the new baby.

I must go back to when I was eight months pregnant with my firstborn. It was a Saturday night. He [Ted] was out boozing as usual. I couldn't go to bed; I had to let him in. I was only allowed one Key, and seeing I went to see my Mam, I had to let myself in. He was late. It was about twelve o'clock. He still wasn't home.

I could not settle, so I put my coat on over my pyjamas and went to the pub, looking to see if he was talking outside.

I'll never forget that night. It was raining heavy. I stood opposite the pub. He wasn't there. Just then, the door to the house part [of the pub] opened and there he was. He had been playing cards with the landlord.

When he saw me, he said, "What the so-and-so are you doing here?"

He pushed me. I slipped and fell on my back. He just walked away and left me to get myself to my feet. When I got to the front door, he snatched the Key out of my hand, opened the door, and then shut it in my face. I crossed over the road and watched him light the gas jet, put it out, and get into bed. So, that was it. It was about one o'clock then. I didn't have far to go to my Mam's. I knocked on the door.

My Dad opened it and said, "What the hell!"

He said, "Come in, Cock."

So, I lay on my Mother's couch all night, not sleeping.

Next morning, which was Sunday, Mam said, "You are not going back to that Swine."

But I did.

I got my sister, Lily, to go with me, looking for him. He was with his Father, pigeon racing. My sister spoke to him. He wasn't pleased.

He took me back to the apartment, and I shall never forget him saying, "Remember, I didn't ask you to come back."

I was so hurt. After, he went out again, to the pub. That's all he ever lived for. Himself.

I cried buckets that day.

Well, life went on. After the birth of my Son, I can only remember being alone. Ted used to go out about eight o'clock in the morning, and maybe I would not see him till about six o'clock at night. And you did not ask questions.

He was that kind of a man.

My life was full with the two kids. I used to take them out in a big coach-built pram. Little Teddy at the top and Audrey at the bottom. If it rained, I used to put them both at the top, under the hood. I only gave ten shillings for it. Second-hand, of course.

Well, would you believe it, little Teddy was fifteen months old, Audrey, eighteen months old, when one night, big Ted came in with one of his mates.

And Ted said to me, "Come around the corner for half an hour."

It was to a labour club. The kids were asleep. Teddy in his cot, Audrey in the big bed. And the girl opposite said she would look in on them.

When I came back, I opened the door. I said, "What on Earth is the smell?"

Audrey had only dirtied the bed, cleaned it up with a pillow slip, put the top sheet over the bottom one, and layed there with her eyes screwed up, pretending to be asleep. Not only that, but she had put the dirty pillow slip at the bottom of little Teddy's cot and blamed him.

The thing I was annoyed about was [that] I had only changed the bed that day and had been to the washhouse.

I thought, "You crafty little bugger."

Well, on the move again. Yes, not long off my time, another baby. Got a better place. This time, mind you, it was always left to me to find the places, and lugging two kids along with me. Anyway, this apartment was on the bottom floor, apart from the one bedroom, which was upstairs, and a downstairs kitchen and a little scullery, which you could walk in and back out, it was that small. Still, it was much better than one room.

It was summer, 1934, and, my, was it hot. And I was near my time when Audrey developed whooping cough. My, she was bad. She used to disturb her Father in the night. He didn't like that. I had to take her downstairs, make her a hot drink. This went on 'till the day [???] arrived, and I went into labour. He [Ted] was still in bed. I was in a state. I was broken-hearted with having to leave my kids, especially Audrey, who was still bad with the cough. I asked a woman I knew if she would look after the kids while my Husband took me to the Hospital.

She said, "Yes, don't worry."

So, I went upstairs and told my Husband I was in labour. He was annoyed at being disturbed.

We walked all the way down to Sefton General Hospital down Smithdown Road. I remember walking behind him as if I wasn't with him. All the way up the path to the Maternity Part, and then he left.

I wasn't in long when I gave birth to another daughter, who I called Rosa Helena, after my Mother.

But what a time I had! The afterbirth wouldn't come away. The nurses, one, of course, would sit on my stomach. I was past caring. I wanted to die. I couldn't cough or speak.

In time, as the days went by, I was propped up, and they were giving me some vile stuff. The afterbirth started to come away in pieces. Oh, I was in a mess. My poor Mam came in with Ted. She looked at me and started to cry.

"Oh, my God!" she said.

She had a bad heart. I must have looked terrible, mind you.

The latter end of me carrying Rosa, in between my groin, I was red raw. I don't know how on Earth I had carried on. No sleep. I had to put wet rags between my legs and look after two kids, and a sick one at that.

No wonder I wanted to die.

*Photo 6. Sefton General Hospital c. 1930. off Smithdown Road. Previously Toxteth Park Union Workhouse.*

W ell, that was number three and another three shillings. Well, the day I went into Hospital to have Rosa, Ted took Audrey and Teddy into Hospital. So, when I came out of Hospital, there were no kids to greet me. But after a few days, the Hospital sent little Teddy home but kept Audrey in. Little Teddy did not get the cough, thank God. Audrey was coming home in three weeks. OK.

I wasn't a well girl after what I had been through.

So, I was the Mother of three children at the age of twenty-one years of age.

I was very depressed after having Rosa. I did a lot of crying. So, when I went shopping, it was two kids in the pram and Audrey, being the eldest, she walked alongside of me, holding the pram handle.

I used to dress them nice, all from the second-hand shop. Very good and smart clothes, all for a few shillings. A shirt for Ted was only a shilling.

My children were my life. I was very happy with them.

The day came when Ted said to me, "<u>Always</u> <u>remember</u>, I did not marry you, you married me."

I thought, "My God, what next?"

I was so hurt. But he meant it. He never once told me he loved me, and he repeated that!

Years after, he said, "I never thought anything of you when you married me. But over the years, I come to think a lot of you."

I think [that] when he told me that, it was like water off a duck's back.

I thought, "Nothing you say anymore can hurt me."

As the years went by, and more kids kept coming. Rosa was two years old when Jean was born. 10 lb 4 ozs. I also had moved to a rented house. My first two bedrooms, parlour, kitchen, and back kitchen. No bathroom or toilet. That was in the backyard. Had a tin bath to bathe the kids in it. By the time Audrey was going to school, Teddy and Rosa were running around then.

I had my troubles then. Three of them with the measles. Rosa, the baby caught pneumonia. Very lucky with her. She had to go into Hospital. But God was good to me. She came out.

Well, things got bad. Short of money. Got into debt over the rent. Owed three weeks. The landlord threatened me with the bailiffs. I had not much of a home, but what I did have I wanted to keep. So, I got an apartment round the corner from where I lived; rooms over a [???] rooms. One big room and two small bedrooms, small fireplace in the middle of the big room, no floor covering. Gas again. Still, it was a roof over our heads. Had to go down about thirty stairs. What a hike! Up and down for water to wash the kids and Ted. By the time night-time came, I was worn out.

Well, one day, Ted said to me, "How do you fancy going out, knocking on doors, asking, 'Have you any old clothes to sell?' I'll take you to the places where you will get some."

Well, I was shocked. Me, so proud. But things were bad.

But he said, "Whatever you get, we will go halves on the profit."

Of course, he was thinking about his ale money, where I was thinking of the kids. So, he took me to Lance Lane; houses with front and back gardens.

First stop was Tulip Road. First door I knocked on, an old couple lived there. I bought a man's suit off them. It was brand new, but the old lady had made a mistake. The pants were too long, and she had cut the bottoms off and ruined the pants. So, I gave her five shillings for the suit along with the pieces off the bottom of the pants. I went back to where I had left Ted. I couldn't go knocking at any other doors because I had no more money, and I had borrowed that off my Mother.

Anyway, we cut through Wavertree Park for home. I took the pants to a tailor to put the bottoms back on, which he charged me five shillings for them. I took the suit to Brown's pawnshop and pawned it for two pounds ten. Fifty shillings. That was two pounds profit. Of course, that was a pound for Ted and a pound for me. I was over the moon. When I paid my Mother the five shillings back, she suggested getting leaflets printed, for me to put in doors, up one side of the road, down the other side, about fifty houses altogether.

On the leaflet, it said, "Cast off clothing bought. Call back in one hour."

Some of the people would slam the door in your face. Those were the toffee-nosed ones. Others were so different, kind and understanding.

I did very well with the buying. I made a lot of friends. That's what a lot of them were to me, not just customers. Ted used to mind the youngest child, but he still got half of what I made. I used to get some beautiful clothes at times. I always used to make plenty of profit.

So, I did that work because it was work. Hard work, and out in all weathers. But I was happy doing it, more food and clothes for the kids. I got them all out of the bag. I dressed them like little Toffs, and for the home too.

Well, all too soon, I became pregnant again. Had to move again. Got a house in Tunnel Road, sixteen shillings a week. Three bedrooms, a parlour, kitchen, back kitchen, backyard, toilet outside. But it was a house. Gas cooker. Gas light, but a big fire range with [an] oven that when you cooked in the oven, you pushed the hot coals underneath it. It was smashing for cooking pies, cakes, and hotpots. And the kettle on the hob, ready to boil.

Well, I had another daughter, who I called Veronica after myself. So, that was five kids, and it did not stop me from going knocking.

I had a stall in the market, and I used to go every Friday afternoon with my eldest daughter, Audrey. She would be about eight years old. She used to carry the case with the clothes in, and I used to carry the baby and a case, too. When we got to the market, I would empty the clothes out of the cases; put the baby in one to sleep, then I could get on with selling my stuff. I nearly always used to sell out. I loved it. The place was so alive, and it cost me four shillings for the rent of the stall. And many a thing I used to pick up cheap for the kids. In the winter, it was cold, but we were underneath cover, so we were not too bad.

Well, time went on, and Vera was twelve months old when Germany was at war with the British. Then things started to happen. Air raids. I had three kids that had to be evacuated. Audrey, Teddy, and Rosa. And then Ted was called up. I was left with Jean and Vera. I got two pounds a week from the army. I had to take the two kids every week and travel to North Wales to see my three kids. Take them some clothes and shoes, and they were half fed. So, I brought them back home.

I thought, "No one is going to treat my kids like that."

Well, the war got worse. Bombs dropping. Gunfire. Frightened the life out of us. As soon as you heard the air raid siren, you started to duck, in case you got one.

My poor Dad took bad. Rolling on the floor in agony all night. Couldn't get a doctor to come out. Had to stand by for the air raid casualties.

We finally got him into Hospital. He was a goner. Two days. Perforated ulcers. What a shock to us all. My poor Mam, she was lost. Speaking for myself, I was overcome with Grief.

I loved my Dad very much.

Well, Mam took to a sickbed with cancer, and while she was ill, she received a telegram from the War Office informing her that her Son, Robert Kay, had been killed in action. Well, she took off screaming. Ran out of the house into the road in her night attire. We all thought she had lost her senses, which I am sure she had.

He was only twenty-six years of age.

Well, Mam started to go downhill, then we lost her. What a loss!

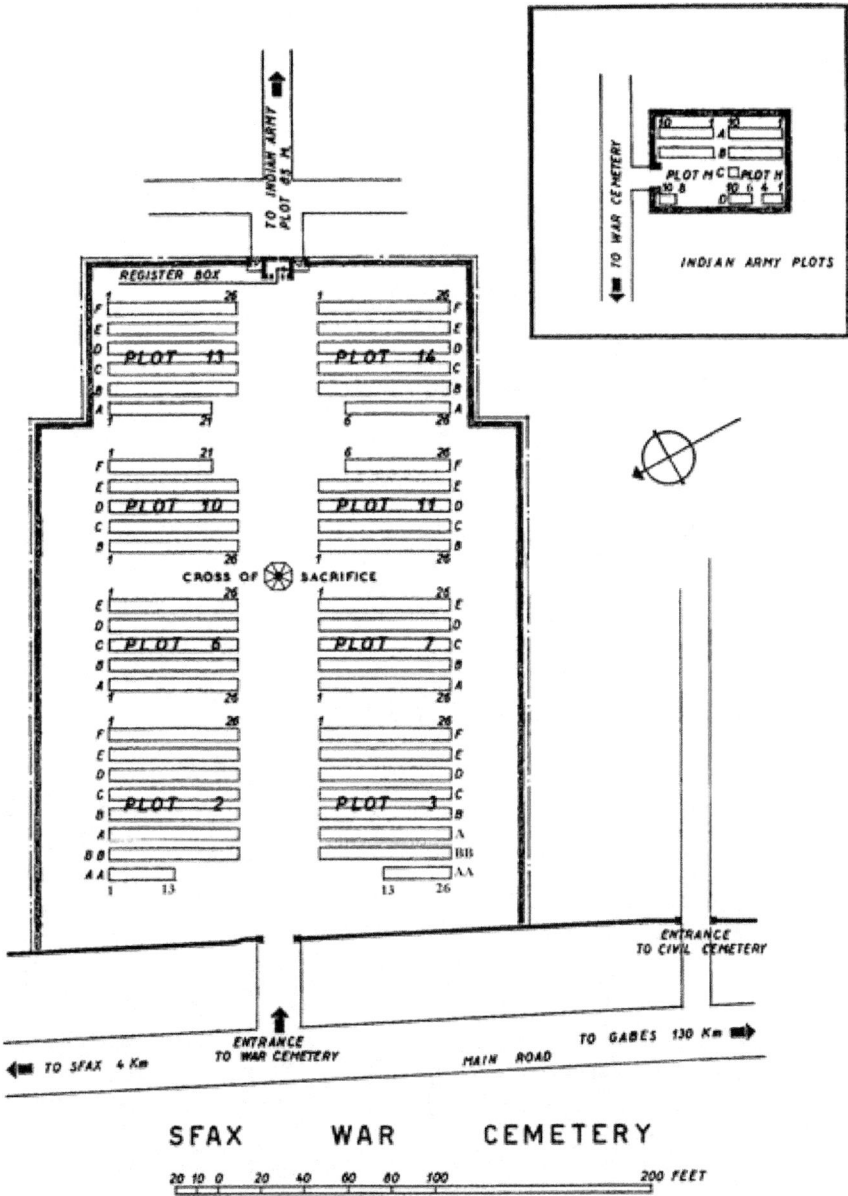

*Image 1. Schematic overview of Sfax War Cemetery where Lance Corporal Robert Kay lies at rest.*

*Casualty Search, Commonwealth War Graves Commission.*

*ID: 2182979*

*Surname: Kay*

*Forename: Robert*

*Initials: R.*

*Age at death: 24*

*Date of death: 10/04/1943, Moving to Sfax*

*Rank: Lance Corporal*

*Regiment: Black Watch (Royal Highlanders)*

*Unit: 7$^{th}$ Bn.*

*Country of service: United Kingdom*

*Service number: 3656464*

*Burial: Tunisia*

*Cemetery: Sfax War Cemetery*

*Grave reference: VII. C. 24.*

*Additional info: Son of James and Rosa Kay, of Liverpool.*

*Photo 7. Photo of the entrance of Sfax War Cemetery, Tunisia.*

The food rationing, trying to keep ends up. It was hard going, but I kept on. We were allocated with clothes coupons. So, my customers, they had the money to spend but no coupons. I had them. I couldn't afford to buy new clothes, so I swapped the coupons for clothes. I did alright, too.

They were happy. I was happy.

Then the war ended. My Husband came home only after ten months. Soon after, pregnant again. Full time baby, and lost it. I went very depressed. Doctor advised me to go in for another child.

Well, that wasn't hard.

I had a daughter, Lita Roberta, and then another one, Linda. And after that, a full time baby which I lost, and my last one, another full time Son, lived seven hours. Had to have him buried. Put him in a shoe box. Cost twelve and six, which I had to pay. He was my last one.

I was thirty-eight years old, Mother of seven live children.

A full time job.

I was worn out and depressed. My eldest daughter, Audrey, she got married at twenty-one. Married in white with her five sisters as bridesmaids. They all looked lovely. Her uncle Ronny, my brother, took the place of her Father and gave her away. Her Father didn't want to know.

That was the kind of man he was.

We had the reception in a hall. Her Husband payed for all the drink and there was plenty for everyone. Also food. My daughter payed for her wedding dress and her sisters' and mine. She had a good job and she saved up for everything.

But with her going, I was lost. I still had to go out knocking. Things got worse, with no work for my Husband.

I must tell you that when my daughter Rosa was sixteen years of age, she took ill. I went into her bedroom, this morning, to get her up for work, and she had been vomiting all night.

When I saw the colour of it, dark green, I thought "I don't like that."

So, I got the doctor in. He said it was most probably her monthly. As the day wore on, she got no better.

I said to myself, "Sod this."

So, I got him in again. He said he couldn't find anything wrong.

I said, "Do me a favour, will you and get her into hospital straight away?"

So he did. I went in the ambulance with her and then the sister in the Hospital, which was Smithdown Road Hospital.

He said, "Come back tonight and we will let you know what's wrong with your daughter."

The shock was [that] she had meningitis. Those days, they were dying like flies with it.

That was 1950.

Well, what a time we all had. The worry over her. She was picking up fine, and then low and behold, she had her 17<sup>th</sup> birthday and two weeks after she collapsed. The next thing, she didn't know what she was doing. She started to dirty the bed. The next thing, they sent for a brain specialist from Walton Hospital, and the next thing, she was whisked off to Walton Hospital for a brain operation. Oh my God, what a time that was!

I thought, "Oh my God, I'm going to lose her."

First time I ever saw or heard her Father get on his knees and pray. Of course, the vicar was there.

I never prayed so hard in my life, "Please God, make my daughter well."

And after the op[eration], she said, "Hello Mam."

"Oh, thank God", I said, with the tears choking me.

So, altogether, it took twelve months for her to recover, and now, today, the year 1989, she is fifty-four years of age and married with children and grandchildren.

So, that was an episode in my life, which her and I and her Dad and her sisters and brother will never forget.

That happened when we lived in Tunnel Road [2?]7.

*Photo 8. Walton Hospital, Lower Lane, Liverpool.*

Well, life went on, regardless, and me flogging myself as usual, knocking on doors, up one road, down the next.

Well, I reached the age of forty, when my eldest daughter gave me the house. She was living in it, was bought cash.

Well, I was over the moon. The house I had always loved. Bathroom at last, and inside toilet and outside one, as well.

I was living there for about twelve months when I got a shop in Tunnel Road. It was a second-hand shop. Rent was cheap. Also, there was a house part to it which my daughter Jean took over, and helped me in the shop.

So, my trade I had been in since I was twenty-three years of age, I could sell to the public. I gave that trade up, after two years, turned it into Sweets and Tobacco and Greeting Cards shop. I did very well. I made a good living at it, and there were no halfs in that for my Husband, but I paid all the debts, fed myself, paid Rates, coal, Gas and Electric bills.

All I got off my Husband was three pounds ten shillings a week. I had my son, who was working. I got two pounds off him for his food. My daughter Vera, two pounds a week off her. And Leta and Linda were going to school. [Lawrence County Primary School]

So, when they started pulling the houses down all around me at the shop, my takings were dropping. And my daughter Jean had got a house out in Walton. Just what she wanted. Four bedrooms, bathroom, four rooms down the stairs. She also had six children.

So, at the age of fifty-eight, I retired.

That was the year of 1971, just before decimalisation came into force. I was very sad at the time. I felt as if my life had ended. That shop had kept me sane. By then, I was alone. All my kids had got married.

So, there was just my Husband and I.

So then I got stuck in and started to do things to the house. I filled my days up like that. I could paint and paper: one thing my Husband couldn't do and 'wouldn't do'. All my kids had nice homes, and now they own their own homes.

I am still in my really first home now for thirty-six years and I still love it. And at seventy-six years of age, I make fancy pillow slips and bed cushions to match. I made all my daughters sets for Xmas presents, and they thought that they were lovely. I also sent a set to my sister Olive out in America. She is sixty-six years of age, the baby of the family. She couldn't believe I had made them.

"Are you not clever", she says.

I have two more sisters and one brother left, including myself, out of nine of us. My sister Ivy, she is sixty-seven. My oldest sister, Lily, she is eighty-six. My brother, he is seventy-nine years old. And to look back and think poor Mam had fourteen kids altogether and died of cancer when she was only fifty-eight years of age and my Dad, he was ten years older than Mam. He died before Mam, at the age of sixty-five.

So, three brothers and two sisters, which were twins, are gone. One twin sister, she died at the age of fourteen with rheumatic fever, and the other twin sister, she died out in Australia at the age of seventy years of age. She left twins, Boy and Girl, and one other Son. They all live out in Australia.

This is going back to my childhood. Happy days and not happy days. But when you were young, you thought you just had to ask and you got it. Not in our house. You took what you were given, and if you didn't like it or want it, you never got the chance to change your mind.

But my life was happy, especially when I was about six years old. My Father owned horses and I was very fond of them. I wanted to be a horse woman when

I grew up. I loved being among them. They held a fascination for me. They were human. You could talk to them, rubbing their noses against you. They were such lovely beasts. They got used to you, and the dogs, my Dad kept three in all. They were guard dogs.

My Dad had thirty horses, a donkey, a billy goat, a wagon, and a governess-cart to take Mam about in it. Also, he used it to do Business, buying and selling horses. He had some beauties. Big Shire horses, small cart horses, and Jerry, to be put [to] the governess-cart in.

Never a dull moment.

My brothers worked for my Father, and on the side of the wagon it said: "James Kay and Sons. Hauliers, Contractors."

Hard working family and no Mistake, and one big Happy Family, till Mam and Dad passed on.

No longer were we the one big Happy Family.

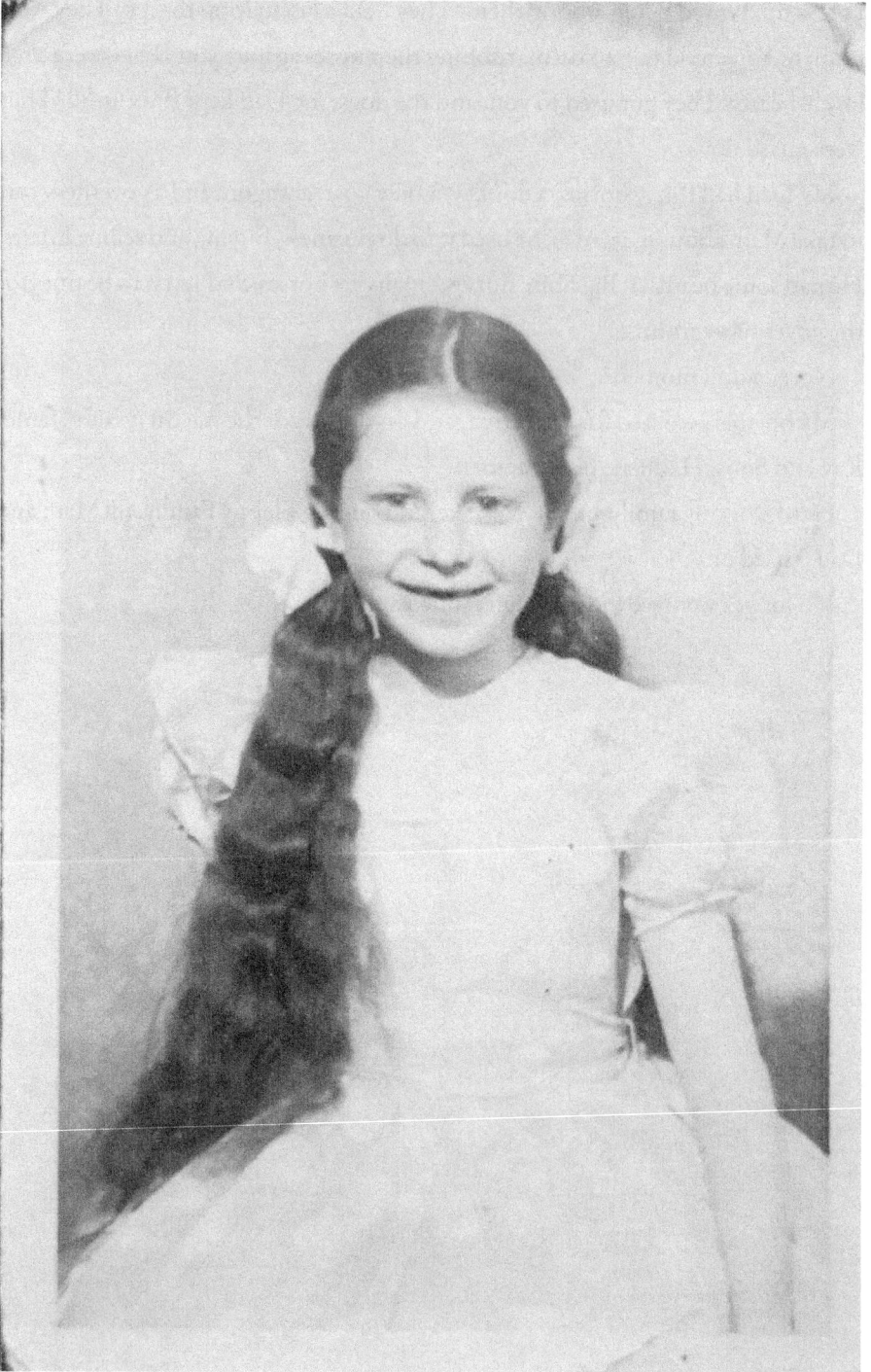

*Photo 9. Young Linda Witham, Mother of Robert Ryan.*

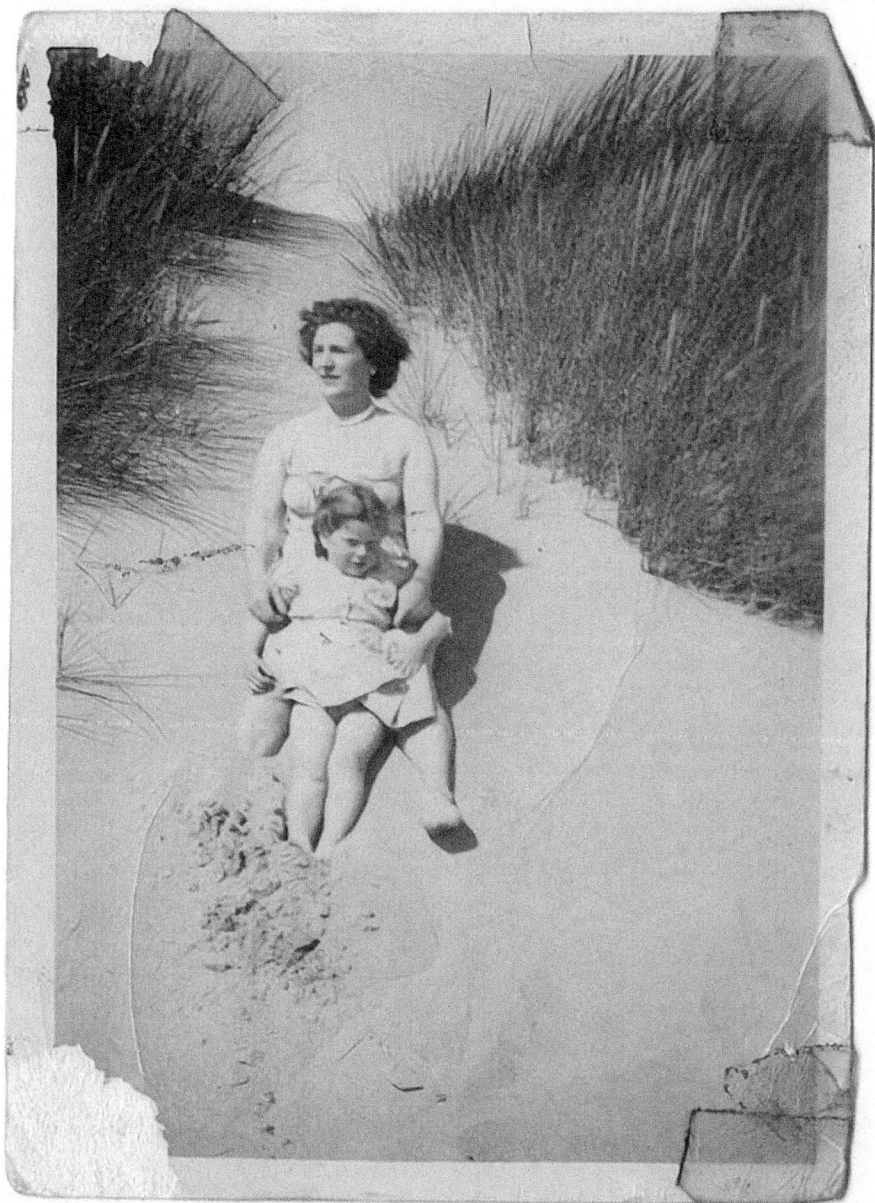

*Photo 10. Veronica Witham and young Linda at Southport Beach*

*Photo 11. Mr Edward Witham, 1960s.*

*Photo 12. Nan, Granddad, Jean.*

*Photo 13. Jean, Annie (Teddy's wife), Linda, Nan*

*Photo 14. Lita, Rosa, Linda*

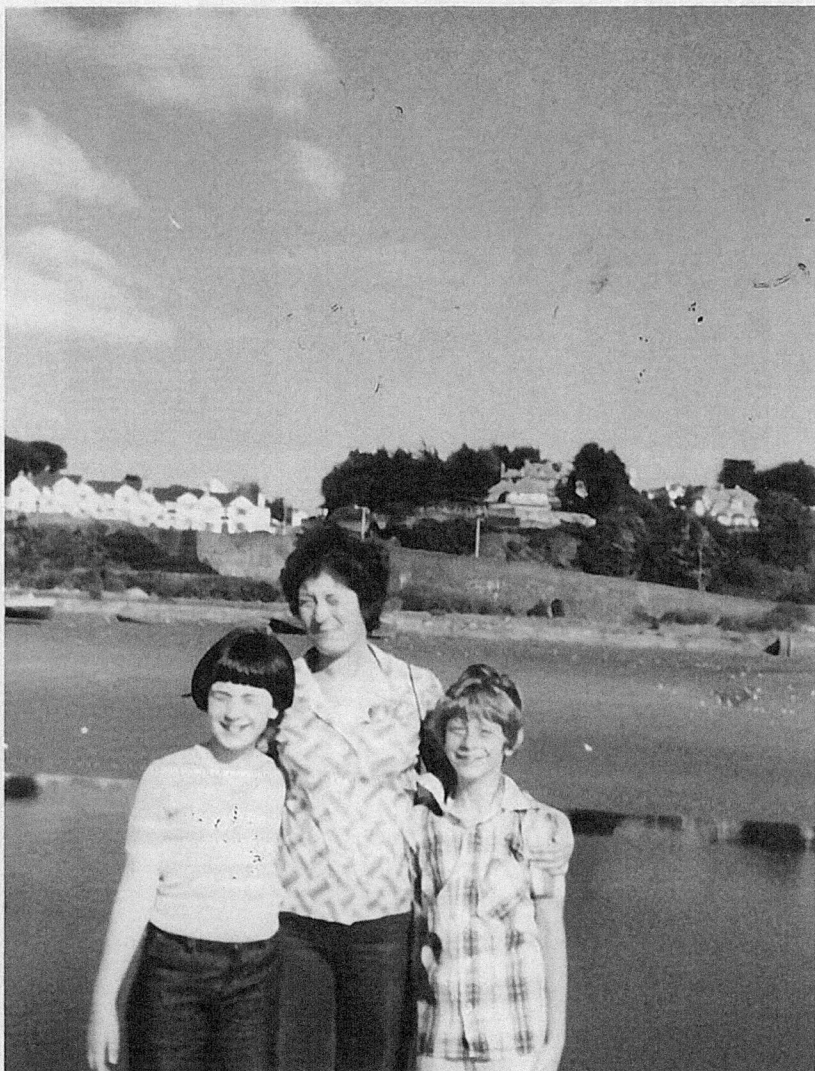

*Photo 15. Lisa, Lita, Robert.*

*Photo 16. From back, left to right, Rosa, Jean, Audrey, Teddy, Veronica Witham, Vera, Lita, young Linda. All of Veronica Witham's living children.*

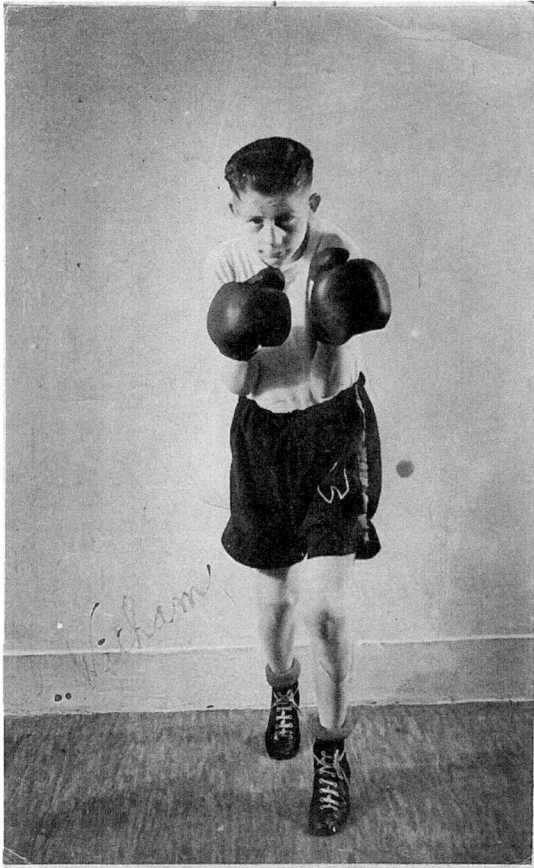

*Photo 17. Edward Witham Jr. Boxed bantam weight under the name of Eddie Kay [his mother's maiden name], born 1932 12 08. Turned professional aged 17 in March 1950, The Stadium, Liverpool, 26 professional fights, W17 L8 D1.*

*Photo 18. The Stadium, St Paul's Square, Liverpool. Built 1932, demolished 1987.*

*Photo 19. Original exterior of The Stadium.*

Well, I think I will go back to my happy childhood days as far as I remember.

I was about five years old when Mam said this day, "Red, school for you tomorrow."

I said, "School? I don't want to go."

I started to cry.

Mam said, "That will be all. You have to go because you are five years old."

What a most unhappy day that was my first day at school.

I did nothing but cry, "I want my Mam."

Teacher, Miss Taggot, her name, she was very kind to me, saying, "Come on, Veronica, you will like it here."

Well, I did get to like it, not a lot. I used to look forward to going home, just to see my Dad with his horses.

We lived in like a big farmhouse surrounded by a big cobbled yard, horses' stalls on each side. Two loose boxers. We had about twelve horses, pony, donkey, and billy goat. Three dogs. They were my Father's life. Horses and dogs.

The yard was full of wagons, a trap Dad used to take Mam out [in], and also used it for his Business.

The pony. I used to curry comb and dandy brush it. He was a beautiful chestnut.

My sister Rosa and I were friends as well as sisters. We went everywhere together, did everything, more or less, together. Mind you, she used to get me into trouble more times than enough with Mam.

One day, I was about twelve years old, I cannot remember what I had done, but Mam had smacked me across the face. I went out into the yard. I was leaning against the wall, and I said to our Rosa, "I wouldn't cry if she hit me on the head with the frying pan."

Our Rosa did no more than go and tell Mam what I'd said. Mam came out.

"Oh", she said. "So you wouldn't cry if I hit you on the head with the frying pan?"

I didn't see any frying pan, but wham, on the top of the head I got it.

"Now cry", she said.

I put my hand over my eyes, and by the way I cried, but I did not. "I'll always remember that."

I hated my Mam and sister then, but not for long.

There was another time, I'll always remember. Mam thought I was fourteen years old, when I stayed away from school. I was on my knees, scrubbing the big tiled floor.

Mam came behind me and said, "Put some elbow grease on it.

I said, looking up at her, "I have none Mam. I've only got soap."

Anyway, while I was doing the floor, someone came into the yard, and I heard Mam laughing. About half an hour later, she came into the house and said, "Red, you haven't left school. You are only thirteen."

I got up, half way of doing the floor, picked up the bucket and threw it across the floor.

"I'm not going back!"

Mam said, "Now you can just get down and mop that floor!"

What a mess. I got myself into mopping the floor on my knees, tears running down my face, with temper, because that was what I was, a bad-tempered bugger.

I had red hair.

Another time that sticks in my mind was the day I came home from school, and found Mam rocking herself in the chair, tears running down her cheeks.

"What's the matter, Mam?"

She didn't speak for a minute, and then she said, "It's our Agg, she's dead."

"Oh, no, Mam."

And I buried my head in her lap and cried my heart out. My sister that had rheumatic fever had gone. Fourteen years old. What a sad day that was, and a long time after, life went on, Mam very sad. Find her crying at times. We all knew why. Dad, his face just crumbled. You would think that his face was going to crack.

People show their Grief in so many ways.

Well, when I was sixteen, we moved house. A big house. No horses. No wagons. The trucks took over, so all the horses were sold.

So, Dad went into the haulage business. My brothers worked for him. My Mother loved this big house. Big, wide hall, large winding staircase. The thing about the house, it was made for my Mam.

She would stand at the top landing and look down, just like a star in a film, her black hair piled on top of her head, Spanish style, with a Spanish comb in the back, shaped like a fan. My, she did look grand. Black velvet gown on, with pearls around her neck, welcoming everybody that came to the New Year's Eve party.

My Dad was a Scotsman, and Mam was Maltese, hair and eyes to match black.

Well, today is Easter Saturday, and I was thinking, you know, the way you do. I got thinking of when the kids were going to school.

I'd say to myself, "I won't buy them pumps for Easter. It's always cold at Easter. I'll wait to Whit."

I wasn't to buy them pumps. I'd buy them Sandals from Clarks, much dearer than pumps. And I'll buy the Girls ones in red with white socks, and a navy blue pair for the Son.

So, I did, for the first time, I bought them. I had a few shillings, and at Whit they looked swell. They were well-clothed out of the bag, as I used to call it. So, that made their day and Mine.

And it was hot weather for Whit.

You know, I always regret not telling my Mam I loved her. I needed her so much after I got married. She would shake her head every time she would see me pregnant. I used to go to her with all my Troubles.

She would look at me and say, "Come here, child."

She would put my head on her breast and say, "Go on, cry. Let it all out", and then tell me, "What's worrying you now?"

That seemed to go on for years. So, when she died, I died too.

"What am I going to do without my Mam?"

One word. Lost.

There was no one to take her place. Lost my Dad, and now, Mam. What more heartache. I couldn't take any more, even after she went, and more kids arrived.

I used to cry when I was in Labour, "Mam, help me!"

And she did.

**M**y girls have all had historections [hysterectomies]. They have suffered.

**N**ow, my daughter Vera has had a Major Op. Had the Gall Bladder removed. She has been through it. I worry about her. Please God, take care of her. She is only fifty. Got years in front of her. I cannot bear to think of her in any pain.

My old man is having trouble with his bladder. They say corns on the bladder. Three years now he has been in and out of Hospital. Due to go back in next month, April 17th. He is eighty-six years old, so he is an old man.

So I say.

What now. Just have to wait, but I must go and see our Vera while he is in.

Set my mind at rest.

**S**o, Easter is over, T. G. No different than any other day here. Same thing, day in, day out. You sure get fed up with it. But got to carry on regardless.

Oh, what it is to be able to turn the clock back. Would we be so strong-headed and stupid?

Well, at least I have learned a lot in seventy-six years. And a lot I've learned I don't like, and a lot I <u>have</u> regretted. But it all comes with living.

You live and learn, and by God, I learned the hard way.

So, that's another episode in my life.

Oh, I wish our Rosa would settle down in one house instead of flitting from one to another. She has a beautiful little house and lovely home, but her X Husband who still lives with her wants to sell the house because he wants the £5,000 she owes him, that he put into the house when they first bought it.

So now it is up for sale, so she can pay him back, and she is going to get a rented house.

Well, when it happens, I do hope she will get a place she likes and will be much happier in it. I so hope so.

He wants his cake and eat it.

She never seemed to settle with him. I don't know why he doesn't piss off, but then, again, he knows where his bread is buttered. He's not daft, he just thinks she is daft enough to let him get away with it, running a car which he cannot afford. Just sits outside the front door.

Men, they just have you for doormats.

I worry so much over Vera. I cannot rest. Please, God, be good to her. Let her live. I couldn't bear it if anything happened to her. I just couldn't. So, please, God, hear a Mother. Please, answer my prayers.

I cannot write any more tonight. I feel so down.

April, 14th, '89

Ted playing up again.

I sometimes think, "How long can I go on putting up with it?"

It's like living with a Geakel and Hide. Turns so quick. Got me going [?] it. Sure is getting me down, depressed.

All I want to do is die. Death would be better than living this life. Something got to give?

Thank God, Vera is on the mend. Been a very worrying time.

Ted today has been smashing, really concerned about me this morning, because I wasn't feeling too good. I don't know what's wrong with me. I get so tired doing the least thing, like Hoovering. I feel as if I had been running around the block.

I guess I am old. No other way of looking at it, but it makes life so depressing. Full of aches and pains.

You think, "Where is it going to end?"

It is not living, it is just existing.

So, in the meantime, I am an old woman, and cannot expect any different. Take one day at a time, and thank God that's it.

I look forward to Audrey coming on a Sunday. And Rosa, I don't know what I'd do without her. She is such a help, cleaning windows, putting curtains up, takes me shopping, takes me to the library for my books. She's a good kid.

I worry about her. She is so unhappy. Please God that when she moves house, she will be happy.

What it is to be happy and contented these days. You know, I don't know what I'd do if I had no family. God, I would be alone. I wouldn't be here, that's a cert.

At least I kept them all together. One family.

And when my time comes, I will say, "Thank God for the love of my children, and thank all my children for loving and caring for me."

My daughter Linda and her two boys and her Husband emigrated to South Africa seven years ago. Haven't seen them since. She owns her own house. Has a swimming pool. She has a good job. Private secretary, very good money. Her Husband works in the gold mines. Her oldest son, Robert has just married. She is very happy with her life, T. God. She has red hair like I used to have.

Of course, now I am white.

My daughter Lita, she lives in Newcastle, her own house. Daughter Lisa, Son Johnathan. Lisa is engaged. Got a good job in one of the Forte's Hotels and loves it. Lita's very clever. She does a lot of sewing, always on the go but suffers with her back doing it.

*Photo 20. Veronica Witham, Lisa, young Johnathan, Grandad Edward Witham.*

J ean owns her own house, very nice, big garden. Got it lovely.

A udrey owns her own house, always has. Hers is a beautiful house.

R osa has sold her house and is going into a rented house. She is depressed, has been for three years. Please God, she is going to be happy for once in this house because she has had no bloody luck since she ever got married, and that is three times.

Some people are born to suffer, and she sure has had her share. Like me, since I married at seventeen and am now 76.

What's my life been? More Downs than Ups. No contentment, but I am still here and intend to be here till the end of my Days.

I understand Audrey, she doesn't want to end her days alone. Now me, I wouldn't mind. Who cares at my age, but I still think that he [Ted] will be here when he is 90. Only the good go first. HE SHOWS NO COMPASSION FOR ME OR ANY OF HIS CHILDREN. SO WHERE THERE IS NO FEELING, THERE IS NO LOVE.

You know, my Poor Mam, she died at fifty-nine years of age. She had twelve children. Bill, Lily, James, John, Mary, twins Rosa and Agnes, Ronald, Myself, Robert, Ivy, and Olive. Twelve children, married at sixteen years of age.

My grandmother, she died 1914.

I was born 1913.

My grandmother was Maltese. Her Father, my great-grandfather was Maltese. But my grandfather was a Preston Man. He died before my grandmother. Grandmother only had three children, Margarette, William, and Rosa.

My Dad was born in Paisley, Scotland.

I remember when I was three years old. Big day, Friday, pay day. I would sit on the top step waiting for my Dad to turn the corner of the road.

He would say, "Hello Cock, are you no waiting for yer wee meg?"

That was halfpenny, two ounces of sweets for that wee meg. That was once a week. I can remember that as if it was only yesterday.

Strange how some things stick in your mind.

My Dad knew the actor, Bill Cody. Buffalo Bill they called him. My Dad read all of his books, all westerns.

Please God, do make our Vee fit to come. I am so looking forward to having her here with me on her own for a few days. I will look after her. Please God, do be kind and merciful.

It will be a relief when Ted goes in [Hospital]. He does nothing but moan. It's piles now that's the daily topic. I hope to God the Hospital do him for them. If it's not one bloody thing, it's another.

Rosa and I have taken him out to the park in the wheelchair. No easy task. He is 13 stone. He is bloody heavy, but he doesn't care. He is not passing it.

Thank God when next Tuesday comes and he goes in. Some peace.

He won't go to Comeleton[?].

He says, "No, I'm alright here."

Self, first and last.

Only seven more days to go.

Only in two days. Nothing wrong.

It is 10-6 '89.

Oh, God. I feel so down. I do nothing but cry. Whichever way I look, there seems to be a blockage. I try to take an interest in things around me, but that seems to be an effort. Even my small garden this year is nothing. I am feeling old, so old. I don't want to go on, there is nothing anymore. I feel so alone at times, so depressed, between one thing and another, I don't know where to turn.

My kids don't seem to understand me anymore. I don't think they want to. They are all wrapped up in their own lives, their homes.

After all, they are saying "Mam's old."

In other words, I've lived my life, they are going to live theirs.

Well, that's life, but in my book, I have not <u>lived</u> My life. I have existed, pushed my way through life, with all the hoard giving Grief, worry, sorry, and a lot of heartache. It's left its mark, not only in my face, but in my Heart, which, at the moment, is very heavy. Tears won't even ease the pain.

God, another day dawning.

Why do I torture myself. It won't make things any easier. I need a break away from it all, on my own. On an island with nobody there, only the birds and the sea. Music to my ears, to listen to the waves dashing up against the rocks. Oh dreams. They never come true.

Well, another day.

Took Ted to get his eyes tested by a specialist, which cost £50, also bifocals in his own frames, £38/50. I sure do hope he will be able to read his paper when he gets them.

Take him to the Royal on the 20 7 89 for a bar eel meal [barium meal] to see if anything is there which is causing inside. Piles.

Christ if it [is] not one thing, it's another.

Now, for days, it's his shoulder.

Never a dull moment here.

I am so weary at the end of the day. I am glad to crawl into bed.

Thank God, Vera is on the mend. She does sound marvellous. I am so relieved. At times, I think God is so understanding. I talk to him. I implore him to look after my Kids. To please not to let anything happen to them.

Take me before anything happens. I just could not bear the love. God, help our Lily, she feels the loss of Agg so much.

What is it to be Mother?

It's one hell or a trial, believe me.

It's 20 11 89

It was on a Tuesday in August 1989. I was in the kitchen. I'd peeled Potatoes for dinner and was making a custard for Ted's tea, when he came into the kitchen and said, "My throat is dry."

I said, "There is some tea in the pot. Put a light to it."

He lifted it up with his left hand, put it down on the draining board, and next he was beating me up with his fist, banging my head, my mouth.

He thought he had left me for dead. I fell over the rocking chair. He thought he had killed me.

He ran out into the road where we live and told a man his wife had had a fit. Of course, when the man saw me, he called the police.

Ted was taken away and put into Mossley Hill Hospital for Geriatrics. He had flipped his lid.

That's four months ago, and now he has given up.

He no longer wants to live.

What a terrible state of affairs. I am out of my mind. <u>I'm</u> <u>alone</u> for the first time in 59 years. I have been with him since I was 17 years old, and now, I am lost. What am I going to do? I just don't know.

I cannot see my life without him, although he is 87 years of age. He has lost so much weight. It's unbelievable, to go from a big Vain Man to nothing. It's heart-breaking to see him.

All I ask of God, is please don't let him suffer.

Take him in his sleep.

OH God, please help him and Me.

My only Wish is I wish life had been different. If only he had been different, life would have been so much happier.

Now it's late for both of us. God help you Ted, in your hour of need.

Your Wife, Vee

It's 1995

I have not long come out of Hospital with salmonella food Poisoning. God, I felt ill. I didn't think I'd make it.

Pity, I did.

Then 2 weeks later, I developed shingles under the Bust. God, what pain. Thank God, it's better. But with having them both, it has left me weak, and the sugar in my blood is up and down.

I am tired all the time. All I want to do is sleep —— I am so fed up with myself.

Tomorrow, Sunday, I am going to stay with my Daughter Audrey. See if that will buck me up some.

I could do with a miracle.

**[FIN.]**

*Photo 21. Audrey, Rosa, Veronica.*

*Photo 22. Mrs Veronica Witham, Copenhagen 1998.*

out in Watton just what she wanted. Four
bedroom bathroom, four room down stairs she
also had Six children. So at the age of Fifty eight
I retired, that was the year of 1971 Just Before
decumilation came into force, I was very sad at
the time, I felt as if my life had ended, that
shop had kepted me sane, by then I was alone,
all my kids had got married. So there was just
My Husband and I; So then I got stuck in and
started to do things to the house, I filled my days
up like that I could paint and proper, one thing
my Husband couldnet do (and wouldnet do,)
all my kids had nice homes, and now they
own there own homes. I am still

# List of Family Members

**Primary Family Members**

Veronica Kay / Mrs. Veronica Witham (1913–2007) – narrator and memoirist; born Veronica Kay; wife of Edward Witham; Liverpool mother.

**Edward "Ted" Witham** (aged 87 in 1989) – Veronica's **husband**.

Children:

| Name | Relationship | Approx. Birth Year / Notes |
|---|---|---|
| **Audrey Witham** | Eldest daughter | Born Sept 1931 |
| **Edward "Teddy" Witham Jr.** | Son | Born Dec 8 1932; boxed as Eddie Kay |
| **Rosa Helena Witham** | Daughter | Born 1934 |
| **Jean Witham** | Daughter | Born c.1936 |
| **Veronica "Vera" Witham** | Daughter | Born c.1938 |
| **Letitia Roberta "Lita" Witham** | Daughter | Born mid-/late 1940s |
| **Linda Witham** | Daughter | Youngest surviving child; emigrated to South Africa; birth c. early 1950s |

**Veronica's Parents and Siblings**

| Name | Relationship | Life Dates / Info |
| --- | --- | --- |
| James Kay | Father | (c.1880–1945) – died aged 65 |
| Rosa Kay (née unknown) | Mother | Maltese; died of cancer aged 58 |
| Lily Kay | Oldest sister | Born c.1903; aged 86 in 1989 |
| William "Bill" Kay | Brother | — |
| James Kay (Jr.) | Brother | — |
| John Kay | Brother | — |
| Mary Kay | Sister | — |
| Rosa Kay (sister) | Sister (twin) | — |
| Agnes "Agg" Kay | Sister (twin) | Died aged 14 of rheumatic fever |
| Ronald "Ronny" Kay | Brother | Gave Audrey away at wedding |
| Robert Kay | Brother | Lance-Corporal, KIA WWII (1919–10 Apr 1943) |
| Ivy Kay | Sister | Died aged 67 in 1989 (b. c.1922) |
| Olive Kay | Sister | Youngest; died aged 66 in 1989 (b. c.1923) |

## Scottish National War Memorial

# Remembered with honour in the Scottish National War Memorial

**L Cpl Robert  KAY**

**THE BLACK WATCH (ROYAL HIGHLAND REGIMENT) and THE TYNESIDE SCOTTISH**

**10th April 1943**

Who gave their life whilst serving their King and country

Chairman of the Trustees

# Afterword

In the quiet margins of her domestic life, between 1989 and 1995, Mrs. Veronica Kay, my dear Grandmother, wrote down her honest thoughts and recollections in an A4 notepad, which she entrusted to me for safekeeping in 2003. I now share her memories, with her permission.

She begins her story in 1930, the year she married, but she also includes moments from her childhood. I have faithfully reproduced her words here, making only minor adjustments to spelling and punctuation.

The short entries are matter-of-fact and unadorned, without flourish or fantasy. Just as she was. Written in the privacy of her bedroom before she retired for the night, they offer forthright, unfiltered glimpses into working-class life in Liverpool across decades of hardship, motherhood, war, and quiet endurance. Her story is simply memory, arriving in those dark hours before sleep.

The attentive reader may notice spelling quirks or unfinished thoughts. But often a single sentence bears the weight of years. In the simplicity of her words lies a quiet emotional power: memories of her graceful mother, the price of clothing, the value of work and self-reliance, and a husband's wage measured in pitiful half-crowns and shillings. She writes of family, illness, war, loyalty, and loss. However, she never relinquishes her dignity or her hope.

I like to think that the ten years she lived after setting down her short memoir on Kenmare Road were gentler, happier years. My grandfather, Edward Witham, passed away after a struggle with dementia, and with his passing, she was free to follow her own interests unencumbered. She moved to a semi-detached house on Renwick Road in Walton, Liverpool, close to her daughter Jean (and Uncle Joey) and her son Teddy (and Aunty Annie). Surrounded by family and only a short walk from the shops on Walton Vale, my Nan spent her final years as an independent woman, respected and loved by her surviving children and numerous grandchildren.

This humble publication is not only a tribute to one extraordinary woman, but to a generation of working-class Liverpudlian women whose stories have often gone unwritten. In preserving my Grandmother's quiet voice, I hope to honour them all.

I offer this afterword with love and gratitude.

To my Nan.

RIP

Dr Robert Ryan

*Photo 23. Nan and Robert in Sweden (1998)*

*Photo 24. Nan and Robert after her operation Liverpool hospital. She recovered and was fighting fit once again. (1997)*

*Photo 25. Nan at home with her dog PET (1993)*

# Also by textworkshop

A Harry Sinclair Cozy Mystery series:

*Shadows of Serenity*

*Moonlit Secrets*

*Whispers of Lotus Villa*

A Bestseller in Travel Humour:

*The Crinkle Crankle Wall: Our First Year in Andalusia*

*A Hoopoe on the Nispero Tree: Our Andalusian Adventure Continues*

*Olive Leaf Tea: Time to Settle*

If you have a manuscript or a family diary that you'd like to bring to life, get in touch via email dr.robert.ryan@gmail.com or social media @sabina.author

Printed in Dunstable, United Kingdom

70719671R10048